# THE FIXED-SPOOL REEL

# THE FIXED-SPOOL REEL

by

PETER TOMBLESON

LONDON : HERBERT JENKINS

*First published by*
*Herbert Jenkins Limited,*
*3 Duke of York Street,*
*London, S.W.1*
1961

© PETER TOMBLESON 1961

MADE AND PRINTED IN GREAT BRITAIN BY
JOHN GARDNER (PRINTERS) LTD.,
LITHERLAND, LIVERPOOL, 20

# CONTENTS

## AUTHOR'S FOREWORD

In writing about the fixed-spool reel I know that I am touching upon an item of tackle which to many anglers is something of an abomination. There is still a good deal of prejudice, especially among game fishermen, against the reel because it helps even beginners to achieve great accuracy in casting.

Because the reel is frowned upon in some quarters and even barred from certain waters some coarse fishermen are critical of it. They maintain that it is so easy to cast with a fixed-spool reel that no practise is needed and even a child can quickly learn to handle one. To my mind this in itself is the reel's greatest recommendation for I do not subscribe to the odd point of view which holds that unless a reel is difficult to handle and master it is not worth using. I am a devoted admirer of the centre-pin reel which I use frequently and which I love to handle but I have long since recognised the place in fishing which belongs to the fixed-spool reel, a reel which was designed for a definite purpose; to enable an angler to cast light tackle long distances with accuracy.

The reel has now well established itself as an essential item in the equipment of the all-round practical angler and has to its credit many fine angling performances and more than one British record fish.

This little book is not intended for the fixed-spool reel expert of long standing, nor is it intended to tell you how to catch fish. It is mainly for the beginner and the average angler who may need some advice and guidance in the use of his new reel.

*Peter Tombleson,*
*Peterborough.*

# CHAPTER I

## INTRODUCING THE REEL

MOST anglers are by now aware of the history of the fixed-spool reel, how it came into being and has since been developed and perfected. The amazing thing about this type of reel is that since the day it was first marketed over half a century ago it has not changed very much; the basic principles built into the reel are the same now as then.

The reel was first offered for sale in 1905, the invention of Alfred Holden Illingworth, a Bradford business man in the wool trade. The bobbin used in the woolen industry was the basis for the spool of the reel but Illingworth's invention was undoubtedly accelerated by the appearance at that time of a reel invented by Leeds' angler Harry Carr.

Carr invented for his own use as a trout fisherman a reel which could be fitted to the rod as a normal centre-pin and then could be adjusted in a socket to turn through 45 degrees so as to allow line to be thrown off easily.

The late J. H. R. Bazley, also a Leeds man and an associate of Carr, co-operated with Illingworth in the production of the Illingworth No. 1 which performed outstandingly at an international tournament three years after its introduction.

In between the first Illingworth reel and the second, the No. 2 which appeared in 1910, came the Chippendale reel, invented by Tommy Chippendale, of Otley. The spool of this reel remained horizontal throughout casting and recovery and it was offered at 15s. with three different sized spools.

Then came Illingworth's No. 2 with a spool similar to the Chippendale and a price of 35s. (less than the first reel). Later these reels were improved tremendously and at the present time we have fixed-spool reels which are beautifully engineered and refined to the extreme. Because of the number of fixed-spool reels available on the Continent, for example, the angler has now a wonderful choice, perhaps too wide a choice. Unfortunately, in this country there are still only a comparatively small number of different types of reels available. It is to be hoped that this state of affairs will be remedied eventually.

## MECHANISM

The mechanism of the reel is fairly straightforward. In the old days the line would often be wound on to the drum or the spool by the movement of the drum itself. This would rotate with the handle of the reel and the line would be wound on to it through the pick-up arm which would be merely an arm of metal with a twist at the end through which the line would run. When a cast was made the finger would pick the line out of the metal eye and replace it for recovery. One of the most popular reels using this principle was the Allcocks Stanley which I have seen used quite recently in a fishing match and with excellent results. The pick-up arm of this reel moves in and out to spread the line on the drum.

The modern practice is to have a stationary spool, that is a spool without a rotary movement, and the line is then wound on to the spool by the rotation of the pick-up arm which encircles the spool. The problem of line distribution on such spools is important and now the spool moves in and out as the handle of the reel turns, evenly distributing the line over the spool.

Further spool development has brought about "banking" in the spool construction so that line will shoot off easier. This means that the actual spool or spindle is thicker at the end nearer the reel, as in diagram one. If, in addition to this, the outer lip or forward lip of the spool is turned down the line will fall off it easily. This is also shown in the same diagram.

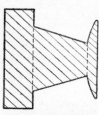

REEL SPOOL SHOWING
SHAPED SPINDLE AND
TURNED LIP

Fig. 1

The interior mechanism of reels varies. Some have hard plastic gears and others utilise metal but the majority now have the mechanism to give forward and backward movement of the line drum so that line through the pick-up arm is

evenly distributed. This is done by incorporating
a reciprocal arm in the driving shaft assembly.
This arm is connected to a shaft which is in turn
connected to the drum. As the arm moves forward
and back with the movement of the reel handle
the connecting shaft imparts this movement to
the line drum.

The pick-up arm of the fixed-spool reel is now
usually what is termed a full bale-arm pick-up,
that is, it describes a half circle joined at both
ends to the housing of the line drum which rotates

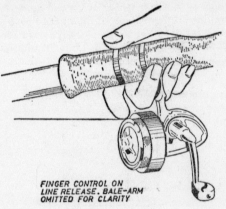

FINGER CONTROL ON
LINE RELEASE. BALE-ARM
OMITTED FOR CLARITY

Fig. 2

with the reel handle. For years the patent covering
full bale-arm was held by a British firm but since
the patent expired other firms have incorporated
this in their reels which previously were obliged
to have halfbale-arms. The latter were quite
successful but they did allow line on occasion to

become doubled round the bale-arm, an impossibility with the full bale-arm pick-up.

Reel handles and reel mountings vary considerably and although we now have reels which offer either right or left hand wind there are few reels which offer any adjustment of reel seating on the rod. Most anglers prefer to fish and use the reel with a handle on the left hand side because when netting fish this allows the right hand to hold the rod and reel while the left hand takes on the job of secondary importance, holding the landing net. But there are some anglers who prefer right hand wind reels and so it is useful to be able to have a choice. Such refinements, however, increase the price of the article and the cheaper reels cannot offer these.

It is also important that the position of the reel on the rod can be changed if required and that the reel can be placed closer to the rod if necessary. Some anglers have small hands and find that the majority of fixed-spool reels stand off the rod at too great a distance for easy use. I know of only one British reel where the position of the reel can be altered usefully.

## SUGGESTIONS

Perhaps it would be too much to expect perfection but if I were able to list the salient features of the perfect reel they would include the following:-

(a)  Right or left hand wind.

(b)  Adjustable reel seating to give different heights and a narrower angle to the rod for ease of line movement from spool to first rod ring.

(c) Roller assembly in the crook of the automatic pick-up arm so that the line passes over a roller and friction is reduced resulting in less wear on the line and the roller.

(d) Handle with positive action and no risk of collapse under pressure. Too many handles have a certain amount of "play" in them when new and this movement increases with wear.

(e) Line drum with expanding spindle to reduce the amount of backing required when using light lines.

Quite obviously a reel incorporating such refinements would be expensive but there is undoubtedly a tremendous demand for fixed-spool reels and this demand should, one imagines, help reduce the cost of the finished article.

## CONTINENTAL REELS

Many British anglers, not entirely convinced of the supremacy of British reels, buy reels which are made on the Continent where they have a wide choice. I am not sure that my list is complete but I have compiled a list of Continental reels which I have put down here for the benefit of those who are interested in foreign reels. I have not examined more than a few of these so that I cannot vouch for their worth at all. On the whole I am impressed more by British reels than by foreign reels which, with a few exceptions, seem to adhere to a rather clumsy overall design. Here is a list of Continental fixed-spool reels:-

| | |
|---|---|
| Alcedo No. 2 (Italian) | Alder No. 4 (French) |
| Abu 999 | L'Arizona (French) |
| Ariston (Dutch) | Alligator (Danish) |

Benora (Swiss)
Benora Coast (Swiss)
Blue Flash (Dutch)
Cargem (Italian)
C.A.P. (French)
Dam Quick Super
Dam Quick Standard
Fix-reel (Swiss)
Kneubuhler-Trick (Swiss)
Luxor Mer (French)
Luxor-Supreme (French)
Luxor-Saumon-Mer-Leger
(French)
Mepps Baby-Vamp
Mepps Vamp-Ousan
Marine Record (Swiss)
Milinello super Niagara
(Italian)
Nylisto
Rileh-Rex (Germany)
Record (Swiss)
Record Special (Swiss)
Tir Tou (French)
Triplex Kaiser
Winio (Dutch)
Sangi-delfino (Italian)

Berna (Swiss)
Benora No. 7 (Swiss)
Bretton 804 (French)
Centaure Pacific French
Dam Quick Finessa
No. 280
Dam Spinnfix
"JIP" (French)
Luxor (French)
Luxor-Saumon-Mer
(French)
Metro (Swiss)
Mitchell (French)
Mepps Super-Vamp
Mastor Fish (French)
Mitchell Saltwater
(French)
Nettuno (Italian)
Punch (French)
Rileh-Jubilar
(Germany)
Spinette 30 (Danish)
Triplex C-54
Universal Werprol
Zangi (Italian)

This list of 51 reels offered on the Continent does not, of course, include the American reels and various Empire and Japanese reels. The majority of the reels listed are left-hand wind reels and resemble in general design the British reels. In fairness to our own reels it must be said that few foreign firms can offer quality reels at a low price similar to those offered in this country without the refinements of the high priced articles.

## CHOOSING A REEL

Although the number of fixed-spool reels available in this country is somewhat limited when compared with the choice overseas it is important for the angler to know what to look for in a reel, depending on his needs and the type of fishing he intends to do.

Perhaps the most practical point to study at the outset is the position of the reel handles, whether they are right or left hand, because so much depends on the manner in which an angler fishes and the way he uses his hands.

Left-hand reels are by far the most popular and on the Continent few reels are offered with the alternative right-hand wind. This is because it is natural to fish with the rod held primarily by the right hand leaving the left hand free to wind in the reel handle. It is also important that no change over need occur when a fish is hooked and needs to be netted. Naturally if an angler is fishing with a reel which has the handles on the right hand side he will hold the rod in his left hand as he turns the reel handle. If he does this and then wishes to net the fish in the normal manner, that is with the landing net held in his left hand and the right hand controlling the rod, he will find he must change hands.

This is the dangerous part of right-handed reel usage for at the point of change over the fish may run and break off. In contest fishing when time is all important it is sheer waste of time to have to change over and then change back again when another fish is caught.

This does not, of course, apply to left-handed anglers who will fish with the rod in the left hand

and automatically use the right hand for work on the reel. For them it is merely a substitution of hands and no change over when in contact with fish is required.

The right-handed angler who has assimilated the habit of fishing with a right-hand wind reel and must change over during fishing would be well advised to change his ways and fish a left-hand wind reel. This is now accepted practice by the majority of anglers and is reflected in the number of reels with permanent left-hand handles.

There are, however, a number of reels which have handles that can be changed over and these are extremely useful, especially where a reel may change hands and be taken over by someone who is left-handed and wishes to change the handles over. On the other hand there are a few anglers, like myself, who fish with handles to the left when bottom fishing but prefer a right handed reel when spinning for heavier fish such as pike. This is a habit I have fallen into for I find that by using the right hand when pike spinning I can concentrate much more closely on the movement of the handles and thus the speed of the lure than if I am winding in with my left hand.

This is purely a matter of personal preference for it cannot be argued that an angler whose strongest hand is his right hand can play a fish successfully when holding the rod in his left hand so that any angler who tries to do so must risk loss of fish.

The majority of good reels have a line recovery ratio of $3\frac{1}{2}$ to 1 which results in a fairly rapid retrieve. However, it is important when choosing a reel to test the action of the handle. Too many handles show, as I have indicated earlier in my list of salient points, movement indicating slack gearing, a fault which can only become progressively worse.

The earlier fixed-spool reels did not have collapsible handles but were built with fixed handles that were inherently strong. Now most reels have handles which will either collapse or dismantle speedily, an "improvement" which is of considerably more value to the manufacturer who has packaging problems than to the angler who must always feel some slight concern over a handle that could fold up on him when into a big fish. If one could have the choice, then the handle which dismantles completely would be preferred to the collapsing type.

## PICK-UP ARM

There is a good deal of variation in this now although the majority of reels have adopted the full arm, sometimes described as the full bale-arm pick-up, or full bale-arm automatic pick-up. This does not allow the line to double up round the end of the arm as it often did on the reels with the half bale-arm pick-up, especially when spinning.

The action of the pick-up arm depends on the quality of the reel, to a degree. The cheaper reels simply shape the pick-up arm so that it brushes up against the reel and is thereby put into the down position; in fact it is "knocked on". Other reels incorporate a mechanism inside the reel which brings the pick-up arm into action after completion of one full turn round the spool.

Next to the spring which keeps the pick-up

arm working correctly and at the right tension for locking, the most important point on the pick-up arm is the part over which the line runs when the reel is winding in line. (Marked "A" in Fig. 3).

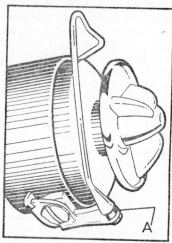

FULL BALE-ARM PICK-UP
MARKED "A" AT POINT OVER
WHICH THE LINE RUNS

FIG. 3

So far I have not discovered a reel which in-corporates into this part any moving bearings. Most reel lines are drawn over this point on the pick-up at considerable tension and there seems little doubt that as a consequence the line itself wears thin and the pick-up metal becomes cor-rugated and contributes even more to the wearing out of the line. This can be clearly seen if a pick-up arm is examined under a low power microscope.

The answer to this constant wear on metal and line is not easy to find but a real contribution would be made if this part of the pick-up arm was fashioned in metal which revolved with the line as it is drawn over it. This point on the arm is the most important point along the whole length of the line between reel spool and hook because of the excessive stress placed on the line which is not only drawn off the reel at an acute angle but is passed over hard metal at an angle which forces the line at this point to an oval shape, a stress which cannot be anything but harmful to the line.

The difficulty the manufacturer would be faced with, of course, in providing a moving part concerns the location of the line on that part. By fairing the present pick-up corner which handles the line he can eliminate any edges which might cut the line but if he introduced a moveable seating for the line it would have to be made so that the line could not slide off. This could probably be managed by using a concave moveable seating wide enough to take the line comfortably.

## SLIPPING CLUTCH

The mechanism of the slipping clutch is probably well understood by most anglers. The clutch is usually operated by application of a tension through a nut on the face of the spool, but some-times it is operated by a screw at the rear of the reel. The position matters little so long as the clutch tension can be increased or decreased fairly sensitively and is easily accessible to the hand.

A number of reels have numerals on the fact of the reel spool close by the tension screw so that when the angler sets the tension he can note exactly the position of the nut, usually marked with a pointer, in relation to one of the numbers. This enables him to find the former tension fairly quickly.

If any stress is placed on ease of adjustment in the slipping clutch it should not overshadow the importance of the clutch itself for if a reel is handled correctly in conjunction with rod action then the tension is altered before fishing begins and if it has been adjusted correctly no further alteration of tension is required during the time the fish is being played. Some authors have suggested that the slipping clutch can be altered when a fish is being played so as to reduce tension or strain on the fish altogether but I do not hold with this view.

The clutch, once set correctly, should not require adjustment, and the action of playing the fish should be done through the rod and the pressure of the finger on the spool.

## SPOOL CAPACITY

Reel spools vary in size and capacity and also shape. I have already suggested an improved shape for a reel spool with the spindle diameter at its greatest near the back of the spool so that line is tipped forward and leaves the spool more easily. Few spools have this refinement but it can be brought about by intelligent backing on the spool.

When choosing a fixed-spool reel spool capacity must be a prime consideration. Nowadays, fortunately, manufacturers cater for all types of anglers and those who require two hundred yards of fine line on their spools will find reels to suit them; so will those who wish to use 150 yards of line capable of holding a carp of double figures.

I believe that spool capacity is more important where sea reels, salmon reels, pike reels and reels employing lines over eight pounds breaking strain for bottom fishing are concerned than for reels which are to be used predominantly for very light lines.

Where a large quantity of fairly strong line is to be used it is likely to be used for most of its length. For example the carp fisherman employing ten pound breaking strain line may well be casting sixty or seventy yards to place his bait and running out up to 120 yards of line when playing the fish. The sea angler may well fish in twenty or thirty fathoms and be using two hundred feet or more constantly.

The light line angler, on the other hand, who is using two or three pound line for roach and bream may not be using more than ten or fifteen yards for most of his fishing so that much of his line is not in use. He is likely to need to discard his line much more quickly because it will wear more quickly so that it is often easier to change over to a new spool of twenty-five yards and use plenty of backing rather than put on a hundred yards of fine line, most of which may not be used for a whole season.

I am, therefore, a firm believer, when using very light lines, in changing lines once a season and starting the new season with a completely new line. I also believe it worth while to change during the season if necessary and would not persist in using a short line well below the lip of the spool if my casting distance was impaired because of this.

The average angler who possesses a modern fixed-spool reel also possesses two spools, one of which he loads with light line and one of which is loaded with heavier line so that he can change if necessary. It is essential that the spare spool should be kept in a dust free condition if possible and, if the angler does not possess a reel bag or box, then a polythene bag will do the trick admirably.

## MAINTENANCE

The reel itself should always be kept in a dust proof container either of leather or polythene so that dust and water are kept out and the reel is kept as clear as possible. In the old days reels were sold in metal boxes lined with felt but now reel bags with a draw string at the neck are favoured because they pull together and are very compact for packing in box or basket.

Reels should be dissembled regularly and oiled as recommended by the makers. It is important in dissembling the reel to ensure that the parts are laid out on a clean piece of paper exactly as they come out of the reel so that the sequence is not lost. If the reel is sold with a paper showing the spare parts this is a valuable guide for taking the reel to pieces and oiling it, for oiling spots are generally marked clearly.

It is useful always to carry a small screwdriver and capsule of oil in case by some accident the reel becomes dusty or wet. It can then be carefully taken to pieces on the river bank and oiled, after wiping the offending material away with a clean cloth or washleather.

Care of tackle, especially reels, pays dividends because a good reel will improve with use, especially oiled use, and after a few years will be run in like a car engine and much improved in movement.

# CHAPTER II

## LIGHT TACKLE CASTING

CASTING light tackle with a fixed-spool reel requires a certain delicacy of touch on the part of the angler. Unfortunately, many anglers find this delicacy difficult to achieve and as a result their casting is laborious and haphazard. Accuracy in the cast is lost and heavier tackle employed to attain, by sheer weight of float and shot, what should normally be achieved with really fine tackle, if the reel and the tackle are correctly prepared.

It is imperative that the angler should decide before he begins to use his fixed spool reel that he will try and use it for what it was designed: the accurate casting of fine tackle. If he wishes to use heavier tackle the reel will also serve him well but if he is unsure of the real purpose of the reel then he will surely flounder in his attempts to make it work.

Thanks to modern engineering science we can now fish with lines of the smallest diameters so that a reel spool will take quite easily two hundred yards of fine line. Naturally, as the line strength increases so does its diameter thus decreasing the amount which will go on a spool. When lines of less than four pounds breaking strain are used it is important to match carefully the terminal tackle and the rod if long casting is required.

25

## FILLING THE SPOOL

Firstly it is essential that the spool of the reel should be filled so that it will work with maximum efficiency when the cast is made. A major fault among anglers is that they fill their spools so that the line, when packed on, is too far below the rim of the spool so that when a cast is made much of the initial energy expended by the angler through the rod is taken up in forcing the line to leave the spool. The further from the rim of the spool the line is then the greater the force required to project the line if the terminal tackle is of the same weight. Fig. 4 illustrates this point.

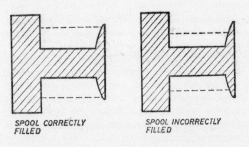

SPOOL CORRECTLY
FILLED

SPOOL INCORRECTLY
FILLED

Fig. 4

As most spools will absorb far more line than the average angler wishes to buy, backing is the solution for bring the line up to the right depth on the spool, usually a quarter of an inch from the rim. The line should be wound on to the reel with the backing attached so that the backing comes up to a quarter of an inch below the rim of the spool. The whole should then be removed and replaced with the backing on first so that the line goes on ready for use.

## BACKING

Backing can be any material which will build up the base for the line. It can be cheap cutty-hunk line, cord or even curtain tape which has the great advantage of being flat and smooth and giving a firm base for the line to go on. Using light lines for roach, bream, tench and similar fish it is not usual for the backing to be unwound from the reel spool, unlike the backing under a fairly short fly line which may well be brought into play when big fish are hooked.

For the angler using heavier lines for, say, carp fishing it is advisable to fill the spool to its maximum with the required line rather than depend on backing.

There is no major difficulty over attaching the backing to the spool but there is something of a problem over winding on to the spool the line from the shop spool. Generally speaking the thinner the diameter of nylon monofilament the less chance of line twisting or coiling so that with lines of extreme thinness it is possible to

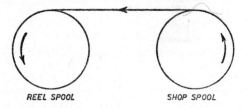

REEL SPOOL                    SHOP SPOOL

wind the line straight on to the spool without fuss or bother. With thicker lines it is advisable to wind the line on without using the bale arm pick-up or the reel. Many anglers when attaching light lines put their reel on a rod butt, secure the shop spool so that it will turn easily and simply put the reel into action and wind the line straight on to the spool.

This action tends to twist the line so that on the reel spool it will lie with an inherent twist that will assert itself as soon as possible. To avoid any twist the reel spool should be taken off the reel and the line should be wound on to it directly from the shop spool as in the Fig. 5. This avoids twist although it takes time to transfer the line. As it lies on the shop spool the line has no twist in it at all; the aim should be to transfer the line onto the reel spool so that it lies exactly as it did on the shop spool.

To ensure a smooth flow of line from the spool when a cast is made it is imperative that the seating of the backing is smooth so that in turn the reel line is evenly placed on the reel. There

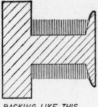

BACKING LIKE THIS
CAUSES OBSTRUCTION

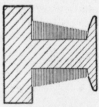

BACKING LIKE THIS
HELPS LINE DEPARTURE

FIG. 6

are several ways in which a stoppage of line can be affected reducing the flow of line from the spool and one cause is unevenness in the packing causing ridging of the line into little hummocks on the spool. If such ridging occurs because of uneven backing beneath the line the flow of line will be arrested slightly when the line is moving off the spool from behind such a ridge. If any ridge is to be built up it should be as in Fig. 6.

We have now backed the line and transferred the line, one of $2\frac{1}{2}$ lb. breaking strain, on to the reel spool. We intend to fish light and wish to cast into the middle of the river, a distance of twelve yards from the bank where we are sitting. Obviously the choice of rod is important so let us consider this item of tackle.

## CASTING

The reel will only work as we wish it when force is applied to the line on it, taking it off the spool in the required direction. This force or cast by the rod must not be too strong for the line so as to cause unnecessary stress on the tackle nor too weak so as not to impart enough energy to the terminal tackle. The force of a cast must be judged accurately by the angler who must err, if he has any choice about this, in casting too hard; for it is possible to check the length of the cast by touch so as to correct over-casting.

The rod should be able to impart the necessary flick so that in general, for punch casting (as it has come to be called) a rod with tip action is desirable. At the same time the rod must be strong enough to take the force from the hands delivering the cast. A rod of whole-cane butt and middle joints with a whole-cane top joint spliced to built-cane is a standard type of bottom fishing rod, irrespective of length, which will cast well with a fixed-spool reel. There are numerous variations of this but for casting light tackle a rod that is too sloppy in action (that is, with an action which extends too far down into the butt of the rod) will result in a jerky cast damaging the tackle, rod and morale. The action of the cast is built around a flick imparted by the upper portion of the rod though this principle does not, of course, apply necessarily to casting heavier items such as spinners and plugs.

The length of a rod is comparatively unimportant so far as the cast is concerned but rod length is important to the angler. He must choose a rod, the weight of which he can manage comfortably. Over the years I have tested and fished with many rods and watched anglers using rods of all types and lengths and there is no doubt that it is impossible to lay down a hard and fast rule with regard to length of rods. A frail, light-handed angler would be at sea with a fourteen foot rod, whereas he would be completely master at all times of an eleven foot rod. If the action of both rods was the same, ideal for the casting he wishes to carry out, then he will do it easily with the rod he can handle most comfortably.

We will choose for the purpose of this chapter a rod such as I have described above, of whole-cane with a tip of built-cane. It has a fairly stiff action with plenty of life in the tip, ideal for our purpose.

If there is one further essential it is that the butt ring on the rod shall be of a greater diameter than the other rings further up the rod. When the line leaves the spool it describes a circular movement spiralling from the diameter of the spool to the diameter of the butt ring through which the line must first of all pass before it travels through the remaining rings. The butt ring in fact reduces the line into something like a straight line and the ease with which it does this depends on the nearness of the butt ring to the reel, the angle between the butt ring and the centre of the spool and the distance out from the rod the butt ring stands.

A competition casting rod will often have a funnel shaped butt ring close to the reel so that the line coming off the reel is quickly reduced to a straight line able to pass through the rod rings easily. It is not practicable to include such a funnel on an ordinary rod but it is possible to assist casting by enlarging the diameter of the butt ring and placing the reel in the most advantageous position.

Unfortunately, fixed-spool reel engineers tend not to consider the mechanics of casting when designing a reel other than to produce a reel which in their view will stand up to hard wear and give reasonable success when handled properly. A good angler can undoubtedly put up a good show with a bad reel but an average angler can put up a brilliant show with a well designed reel and correctly balanced tackle.

For the perfect transference of line from the reel spool into the tube (imaginary) formed by the rod rings the reel spool should be tilted at an angle so that a line drawn through its centre would pass through the centre of the butt ring, or tube

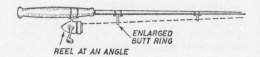

ENLARGED
BUTT RING

REEL AT AN ANGLE

FIG. 7

opening. Fig. 7 illustrates this. Few reels are built
with this angle and if the angler puts his reel well
up the butt of his rod so that his rod balances
better he is often unknowingly prejudicing his
chances of casting well simply because he is
increasing the angle between spool and butt
ring instead of decreasing it as he should.

The alternative, if the reel has no upward tilt,
is to put the reel well down the butt of the rod
and use a butt ring that stands well off the rod.
Because few rods will balance well with the reel
well down the butt this is an arrangement seldom
used.

We therefore set our reel at the position on the
butt where it is handiest for us, having changed
the butt ring so that its diameter is at least double
that of the remaining rings to try and gain what
advantage we can.

## SETTING-UP

To load the line into the rod the bale arm of
the reel should be depressed until it clicks and re-
mains depressed in the open position. The line
will then be drawn off easily. Once enough line
is out so that the float and shot can be attached
the bale arm is brought into action by turning the

reel handle in a forward or winding direction.

An easy running reel can be turned by pulling on the line so that the bale arm moves round backwards giving off line, but this is only good practice where a reel proves suited. If a reel is stiff it is always best to take off line by adjusting the bale arm.

The terminal tackle is then ready and we are ready to make an initial cast.

The cast is achieved in three stages and in order of importance they are simply the aim, the swing, and the release. The former is of prime importance because bad aiming can often spoil good casting simply because the angler is not capable of putting the tackle in the direction he intends. There is no practical means of aiming. One does not sight down the rod or with the thumb held in the air. It is always difficult to describe an instinctive movement (which is what aiming is) but the angler who aims badly is generally looking in the wrong direction and sitting uncomfortably when he casts. It is necessary to be perfectly comfortable and to look at the target.

Most light tackle fishing is done from a seat or basket and the angler does not wish to get to his feet for every cast. He must therefore, be sure that his basket is square to the water and is not rocking with every movement of his body. His feet should be on firm ground so that he can use them if necessary when casting.

Annie Oakley, the famous American markswoman, is said to have described her fantastic shooting in the following words: "I swing, and when it feels right, pull". As every shooting man knows this is exactly how moving target shooting is done; it might well be used to describe aiming when light tackle casting.

Instinct in aiming eventually becomes quite natural, and experienced anglers can generally tell as soon as they have completed the cast whether their direction is right. Direction, or point of tackle entry in the water, is all-important, taking first place over force of cast because the latter can be corrected while the cast is in motion whereas the aim cannot be altered once the cast is made.

The cast itself is a simple operation, when the knack has been acquired. It looks easy and is easy but is best explained in stages.

The first part of the action is straightforward. The tackle should be wound up so that it is hanging down at the required length from the rod tip. The length of line out depends on the depth at which the float is set or, if leger tackle is used, the length of line the angler can best handle to achieve his cast. That will be the length of line with which he casts most comfortably.

In the single-handed cast the rod is held in the right hand. The right first finger takes hold of the line close to the reel spool and holds it tight either against the spool rim with the tip of the finger or under the rod butt in the crook of the finger, whichever is preferable.

The left hand then pulls down the bale arm pick-up until it clicks in the open position.

The second stage of the cast is the swing round of the rod. This should be to whichever side suits the angler best. As the point of the swing is to gain sufficient momentum in the tackle so that a flick of the rod tip will shoot it forward again the

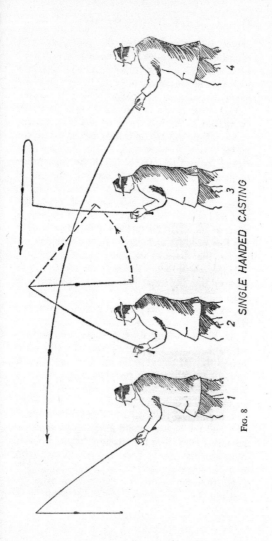

SINGLE HANDED CASTING

Fig. 8

degree of swing, whether the rod goes right round behind the angler, or round to one quarter only, depends on the angler. Generally speaking with light tackle a more powerful drive is achieved when the rod goes well round behind the angler.

The swing round is continued until the tackle swings up either behind or to one side. As the tackle lifts up the rod tip is then flicked so that the tackle shoots forward and, as this happens, the right forefinger releases the line at the appropriate moment. That moment is of supreme importance and must be judged exactly. It becomes easier to judge the time of release with each successive cast and it soon becomes clear that if the line is released too early the tackle will fall down out of the line of sight and may even drop behind the angler. Fig. 8 shows the three stages of the cast.

If the release is too late then the tackle will be plunged into the water just ahead of the angler or may whip round the rod tip and tangle. Fig. 9 shows what can happen by premature or late release.

As in fly fishing it is possible and perhaps advisable for the beginner to watch his line as he swings the rod round in the opening stages of the cast. In fly fishing it is possible to watch the fly line straighten out behind and then turn the head so that exact aim and direction can be attained. The fixed-spool reel cast is a rather faster operation and the angler should always look ahead at his target area when the release of tackle is made, otherwise the flight of the tackle will invariably be to one side or other.

No over-run of line can occur when using the reel but slack line on the water will result if the

RELEASE TOO LATE       RELEASE TOO EARLY

Fig. 9

cast is made so that when the tackle hits the water there is still line shooting off the spool. It is advisable to check this line by the finger tip on the reel spool so that as soon as the tackle is in the water at the required spot the line is prevented from coming off the reel.

Before the pick-up arm is brought back into working position by turning the reel handle forward a check should be made to see that the line is in good order and not tangled in any way. If the reel has been loaded properly no tangle should occur with a normal cast.

If the cast is a bad one, and many early casts will be bad, then the line should be retrieved carefully and the cast repeated. On no account should a cast be hurried. If sufficient distance is not achieved with the cast then more energy will have to be put into it and it may help if the amount of line hanging free is increased giving more purchasing power to the rod tip in the cast.

It is important to check that the line is not wound round the tip of the rod as this will result in tangled tackle and possibly a breakage if a strong cast is made.

The sideways cast with the fixed-spool reel is always difficult from the sitting position, one reason why it is not practised as much as the overhead cast. In a later chapter I shall describe casting for spinning when a sideways action is very effective. From a sitting position the sideways cast often means a premature release of line because, although the rod is travelling in the same direction as the target, the angler is not behind the rod as it goes forward and cannot direct the cast so effectively. It is much more natural to cast

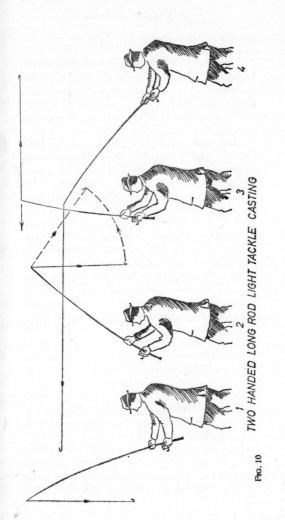

TWO HANDED LONG ROD LIGHT TACKLE CASTING

Fig. 10

directly forward, aiming with the rod tip as the cast proceeds.

The siting of the hands for the overhead cast and indeed the use of one hand or two has been the subject of some controversy among anglers. For casting purposes it does not matter whether the angler is right or left handed. He will develop an action that suits his dexterity.

Some anglers who are very strong in the wrist can cast with a long rod using only their right hand, which releases the line and also guides and projects the rod forward. Most anglers tend to give their right hands assistance by taking hold of the rod with their left hand as it swings round. This steadies the rod and gives additional force to the cast just when it is required. Fig. 10 illustrates how the hands should hold the rod in the long rod cast with light tackle.

This additional push with the left hand has resulted in many broken rods, especially when Spanish reed rods are used. It is not, however, always the fault of the rod. In many cases the angler is using a light, long rod with extreme tip action, a rod that must be nursed to some extent in the early part of the cast. If such a rod must be used for a powerful cast then the left hand should be placed on the rod, as in the diagram, so that it lends support. It is sometimes advisable to lower the reel position further down the rod butt so that the positioning of the two hands does not make for a clumsy cast.

Steel rods and glass rods make ideal casting rods, the former type being probably the most efficient rods in existence to-day for light tackle casting. They are light, have a fairly stiff action and are virtually unbreakable. Glass rods and built cane rods undoubtedly come into their own when using heavier tackle.

Casting directly to the front is an essential in still or slow water fishing where the bait is required to be in front of the angler. There are occasions, such as trotting a fairly fast stream, when it is necessary to cast slightly downstream. The sideways cast can then be used and is remarkably accurate.

The accuracy of a cast can be considerably affected by the prevailing wind so that it is advantageous to fish with the wind assisting rather than hindering. A back wind allows a stronger cast with less energy and even a side wind can be helpful in this way.

Facing winds tend to slow down the tackle as it is cast, restricting the distance which can be achieved. One method of counteracting this is to cast with a low trajectory so that the line cuts under wind. This is not an easy cast but it can be mastered with practice. It is, of course, a low, sideways cast and can be manipulated with one-hand. Assuming the angler wishes to cast across his body from left to right the action is as follows:

The right hand swings the rod across the body at an angle of about 45 degrees, care being taken that the tackle does not foul the bank. The swing brings up the tackle as the rod is flexed for the outward cast and this is delivered with the usual rod tip flick, the line being released by the right hand at the same time.

It follows that one-handed casting like this can only be achieved where the hand concerned can obtain a first class grip on the rod. If the rod handle is thick this will be difficult but if it is thin and easy to grip then one-handed casting should be possible even for the angler with a small hand. It is, of course, advisable for an angler to use a rod, the handle of which he can grip comfortably whatever type of reel he uses. If this hand cannot hold the rod tightly then he will lose control of it after he has been fishing for some time and the hand is tiring. In this cast the rod is held close to the forearm like a splint.

## SHOTTING

We have considered the balance of tackle so far as the rod and reel are concerned. It is worthwhile now to consider shotting arrangements which can help light tackle casting.

The primary purpose of shot on a line is to take the bait down into the water in the manner most likely to assist in catching fish. They are not, of course, intended primarily to cock a float which is merely a bite indicator and a bait carrier on occasion.

Many conditions affect the choice of shotting arrangement, including the way the fish are feeding, swim conditions and the type of bait being used. If the angler decides to fish with the shot arranged to give him the best possible chance of catching fish then he must try and cast with the shot so arranged even though this may not greatly assist in casting.

A string of very light shot, for example, between float and hook gives a distribution of weight that makes casting difficult. If the total weight of this light shot was placed in one large shot at

the extreme of the terminal tackle casting the
same distance as before would be comparatively
simple.

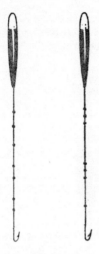

FIG. 11

If wind conditions are against light tackle casting and yet light tackle must be used then the
angler must try and assist his casting by sensible
shotting arrangements. It may be possible to
group shot closer together without upsetting the
balance of terminal tackle that is required. In Fig.
11 two shotting arrangements are shown. The
shot in the left hand diagram is spaced exactly
where it is required by the angler to fish a particular

swim. In the right hand diagram the shot has been grouped together to assist casting without unduly upsetting the balance of tackle.

## FLOATS

The use of a heavy float will, of course, greatly assist casting and this is now possible, thanks to the development of the loaded or self-cocking

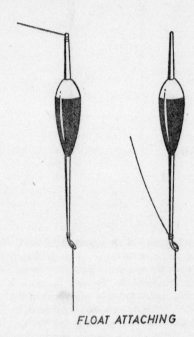

*FLOAT ATTACHING*

Fig. 12

float. This is a float which includes in itself weight which would normally have to be put on the line below it. This is a two-fold gain for the angler can cast long distances yet using only light shot below his float, and as the heaviest portion of the terminal tackle is the float this can be adjusted to be high on the line (as a fixed float) or low on the line (as a sliding float). The angler is therefore offered a choice of shotting arrangements which can greatly assist light tackle casting.

The attachment of the float to the line is a matter of importance because, under certain conditions, a cast can be inefficient if the float is hanging loosely. There are two ways of attaching the float to the line, as in Fig. 12 either by the top and bottom rings so that the float follows at all times the direction of the line, or through the bottom ring only so that in casting the float is hanging loose.

The choice of float attachment depends primarily on the way the angler wishes to fish so that if he must fish with a loose float, and often this is desirable, then he must cast with a loose float. In general loose float casting is not difficult but the tackle does not tend to enter the water so cleanly at the end of the cast as when a float attached to the line at both ends is used. Much depends too on the shotting arrangement. If the shot is heavy and well below the float the shot will proceed first after the cast has been made. If the float is heavier than the shot below it, in the case of the self-cocking float, then the float will proceed first. The only real advantage the fixed float has over the loose float is when it is necessary to over-cast the swim and pull the bait back gently to fall into the groundbaited area. This is sometimes in roach fishing and can always best be attained by using a fixed float, simply because the tackle tends to enter the water hook and shot first so that the tackle is immediately in position for fishing.

The entry of tackle into the water when using a loose float can usually be controlled up to medium distances but at long distances such control is not so easy and the tackle may well enter the water float first with the shot and hook settling down seconds later.

One real difficulty anglers using the fixed-spool reel encounter is when they are fishing very shallow water with tiny shot. This means that they must cast small float and shot which is inclined to tangle up on entry into the water. One shot just below the float may be all that is necessary but the two feet or so of unshotted line can easily tangle up over the float.

Occasionally this trouble can be ironed out when a long rod is used so that the tackle can be cast gently into the water. A loose float on this type of tackle brings the inevitable tangle and if a float attached top and bottom is used the line will still somersault over the float tip.

The answer is quite simply shown in Fig. 13. A spare float top is used with a hole bored through its centre. The line is put through this and the float top fitted on to the float. The line cannot then catch up on the protruding float top. This dodge was used very successively by Horace Storey the winner of the National Angling Championship on the River Severn in 1957 when he was obliged to fish in very shallow water.

## TWO-HANDED CASTS

There is a cast with the fixed-spool reel which is not used widely to-day but which, I believe, will eventually prove very popular. It is the sideways, two-handed cast with the long, bottom

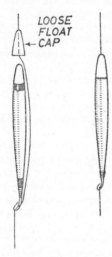

LOOSE
FLOAT
← CAP

FIG. 13

fishing rod. It is a cast practised by a number of top match anglers and because of this merits some description.

Match anglers are perhaps the most accurate of all bottom fishermen when they are using light tackle. They have to achieve accuracy because very often they find their fish in one certain spot which they have groundbaited and, in certain conditions, any deviation of tackle from this spot fails to produce bites and they lose contact with the fish. It is amazing how often this can happen, especially on a water where the fish are slow to feed well and have to be coaxed considerably with accurate groundbaiting.

When this happens the angler knows that unless he can put his bait in the right spot each time he either loses the fish or it takes so much longer for the fish to find the bait.

In either case time is wasted and this cannot be allowed. Neither can the match angler allow time to be taken in over-casting and drawing his tackle back into the right spot. He must be able to hit the spot each time.

Some anglers achieve this accuracy by side casting, others find it more easily attained by over-head casting. The side cast looks easy but is probably more difficult to perfect than the over-head cast because it must be done as the angler sits square to the river and looks at his target. The overhead cast does assist the angler in that there is no likelihood of the swing of the rod unbalancing the angler as might occur with the side cast.

If the angler is right handed, that is, fishing with the rod held in the right hand and the reel handles on the left hand side, he will side cast to his left. The action is as follows:

The tackle is wound up as in any similar cast and the right hand grips the rod at the junction of rod and reel. The right forefinger presses the line to the reel spool or takes the line in the crook of the finger as in the other casts and the rod is swung across the body at a slight angle, about thirty degrees. This permits the tackle to swing to the rear without dragging the ground and does not in any way prevent accurate casting. The right arm is then across the body and the left hand has slid up to grip the rod at the butt above the right hand to lend more strength to the cast. The tackle is swung up behind a line drawn parallel

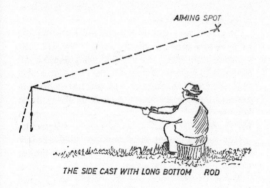

THE SIDE CAST WITH LONG BOTTOM ROD

Fig. 14

from the angler along the river bank to his rod tip and at the right moment the rod tip is flicked to project the tackle out to the river.

The tackle does, in fact, move along the hypotenuse of a triangle formed between the object the angler is aiming at, the rod and the line of flight, as shown in Fig. 14.

If the angler flicks the rod tip to project the tackle outwards without aiming in to a point in front of him the tackle would merely flick out into the river at right angles to the rod tip and would enter the water some distance away from the spot where it was intended to go. The angler must aim the tackle at the spot so that it follows a line of flight aimed from the rod tip to the spot in front of the angler. If the fishing spot is upstream or downstream the necessary alteration will have to be made in aiming.

Line release is normally achieved by using the right forefinger, but some anglers use the left hand to good effect in this case. They depress the automatic pick-up arm with the left hand and hold the line in the fingers of the left hand releasing the line at the right moment. This means that the left hand holds the line away from the reel spool with a pressure against the weight of the tackle, or the fingers of the left hand can hold the line against the rod butt or as in normal practice, against the lip of the spool.

Using the left hand to hold the line and release it does mean that the right hand must take the weight of the rod and provide all the energy for the cast. This is not always possible, especially if a heavy rod is being used by an angler of light physique. If a very light rod can be used then one-handed side casting is not difficult and line release by the left hand often gives excellent accuracy.

The same cast is often used by anglers anxious to cast under-wind and avoid the full force of the wind as they use light tackle. The procedure then is very similar but the angle at which the rod is raised is considerably less than in normal side-cast and this calls for precision so as to avoid contact with the bank.

# CHAPTER III

## PLAYING THE FISH

WE have now mastered the cast. We know what our reel can do and we know how to take care of it. We must now learn how to handle the reel during the time we are fishing so that the reel can be manipulated naturally without any thought.

Anglers brought up on the centre pin reel are inclined to consider that no other reel is quite so foolproof. There is no doubt that for short distance fishing and for swimming a stream the centre pin reel is hard to beat. But it can be matched by a fixed-spool reel when handled expertly.

Once the cast has been learned so that accuracy and distance can be attained easily there is nothing to worry the fixed-spool reel user when stillwater fishing until he hooks and plays a fish. He must watch slack line when casting but this is quickly controlled by finger manipulation which becomes quite natural as time goes on.

## TROTTING

When fishing running water and especially when float fishing or trotting the stream the angler must learn to use his reel while he is fishing. He cannot just put down the rod and remain immobile until a bite is registered.

It is imperative when trotting the stream that the reel allows the float tackle to swim downstream without hindrance. In this respect the fixed-spool reel has an advantage over the centre-pin. If very light float tackle is used with a centre-pin reel then the reel drum must be moved by hand to allow line to be paid off because the float tackle may be so light it will not turn the reel drum by its own weight.

On the other hand if a fixed-spool reel is properly loaded then line will virtually fall off the spool at the slightest tug by the float tackle. With a centre-pin light tackle will sometimes manage to move a very well oiled reel drum towards the end of the swim down when there is a length of line out the weight of which combines with the pull of float tackle and is sufficient for the purpose. Often when this happens as the line straightens between float and reel the terminal tackle is lifted right up from its correct depth.

This cannot happen with a fixed-spool reel unless there is any loop in the line or knot which may prevent free exit of the line from the spool or unless the reel line is set down too far below the rim of the spool.

With light float tackle on the fixed-spool reel the cast into the swim should be followed by a lifting of the rod tip to put out some slack line. This gives the float tackle a certain amount of time to settle in the swim and begin the journey downstream before the line straightens out between float and spool. If the tackle is moving from right to left the left hand will have little to do for the right hand will control the speed of the line from the spool.

The right hand should therefore hold the rod at the reel fittings so that the right forefinger can be near the reel spool ready to check the line when a bite occurs. When the float does show a bite the right forefinger should immediately press the spool rim stopping the line from moving off, at the same time the strike should be made. Some anglers use the left hand for this check, others strike only after bringing the automatic pick-up into operation but they lose time in doing this.

However it is done, and much depends on the dexterity of the angler, the line must be stopped from going off the reel spool when the strike is made. The use of the right forefinger at sight of a bite is generally the best method for fast water where line is peeling off the reel spool rapidly.

In slower water it is possible to trot with the automatic pick-up in position for retrieving, the line being taken from the reel by the left hand which slowly pulls the line and puts the pick-up into reverse to allow line to be taken off.

If the reel is well loaded and light line is being used then the handle of the reel can be reversed slowly as the tackle trots downstream. This is in many ways the most efficient method for trotting if it can be done and is only possible when the spool is well filled and a thin line is being used. A thicker line tends to spring off the reel as the handle is reversed and there is little pull from the float to keep the line straight.

The advantage of reversing the reel handle lies in the fact that the left hand is already where it needs to be for playing a fish or retrieving line and the pick-up arm is in position for retrieving.

It is essential that a reel with a smooth action

be used for this and that the angler checks carefully the movement of the line from the reel in case of stoppages by loops or knots on the line.

In very wet weather rain will penetrate behind the line drum of the reel and may cause friction in the bearings so that smooth action cannot be maintained. This should be watched carefully.

## PLAYING

A great deal has been written about playing fish with a fixed-spool reel, much of it complete nonsense which has completely misguided anglers so that they have never been able to use their reel properly and have been put off because of a succession of lost fish.

Among the many misleading suggestions one finds are the following:-

The tension of the slipping clutch must always be set to just below the line strength.

If you wind in a fish with the slipping clutch working you will never lose the fish.

As a fish pulls at you wind in line and rely on the clutch to stop line breakage.

Don't bother with the slipping clutch but wind it as tight as it will go and forget about it.

The above suggestions should be completely disregarded by the reader. What should be remembered is that the slipping clutch is a device which gives the angler a great advantage over the fish if properly used.

Why is there such a thing as a slipping clutch? To reason out why the clutch is essential we must look at the original type of fishing reel, the centre pin reel. Because of the fact that the centre pin reel acts like a wheel facing the fish, line can be given off extremely easily provided all checks are removed. As the fish pulls, the spool revolves and gives line.

But the fish cannot be allowed to run free and take all the line he wants otherwise he would snag or take all the line out and simply break when the line came to an end. Therefore a check must be put on the fish. In the centre pin reel this check on the rush of the fish, which is intended to make the fish fight hard for any line he gains and thereby weaken him until he can be netted, is generally given by the fingers which act as a brake on the drum through pressure. This is the perfect form of brake.

Now because of the position of the reel spool in relation to the direction line goes out from the rod, the fixed-spool reel cannot work exactly as the centre pin. The spool can, however, revolve and give off line as a fish pulls even though that line does not go straight from spool to fish but goes through the bend in the pick-up arm.

It would be possible to design a fixed-spool reel with a set clutch tension which could not be altered. In many ways this would be an improvement for some anglers who simply ignore the clutch anyhow. They would then be obliged to try and understand it.

## SETTING THE CLUTCH

As it is the clutch can be adjusted so that the amount of pressure required to move it varies. Obviously the pressure required to move it must be less than the breaking strain of the line otherwise as soon as a fish pulled and the clutch did not slip the line would break. But the line strength is not the deciding factor, rather is it the action of the rod.

First principles of playing a fish demand that the rod must be raised upwards and not lowered so that the action of the rod can work correctly.

The clutch tension should be set so that when the fish pulls hard when the rod is at the right angle for playing the fish line is given off, and the spool revolves. The angler should then prevent line from being taken by braking with the finger on the spool rim, just as one would with a centre pin reel.

The action after striking the fish and hooking

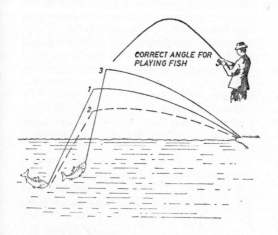

CORRECT ANGLE FOR PLAYING FISH

FIG. 15

it is that the rod assumes the right position, a
little higher than 45 degrees, so that its full action
is felt. Line will be taken off the reel as the fish
pulls and the clutch slips and the angler's finger
brakes the revolving spool when necessary. The
rod tip should be lowered slightly and the line
should be retrieved by winding the reel handle
at the same time. If the fish rushes off again line
will be lost through the slipping clutch but again
the brake can be applied by the finger and retrieved as the rod tip is lowered. The action for
playing the fish is shown in Fig. 15.

If line can be retrieved then the rod tip is brought
up again in a pumping movement and then
lowered again so that line can be brought in.
This pumping process is repeated with the fish
expending his energy through the slipping clutch
from time to time until it can be netted.

Very often a fish will run hard and take line off
through the clutch and then turn before finger
brake action can be applied. If so the rod can be
lowered and line retrieved quickly as the opportunity presents itself.

It is, of course, useless to wind in while a fish
is taking line because no advantage is secured by
the angler and there is danger of line breakage.

The accurate setting of the clutch tension
depends on the action of the rod. The stiffer the
rod the greater will be the tension provided that
it is not greater than the breaking strain of the
line. The best way to set this tension is to hook
some object on the bank and raise the rod until
it is in the correct position for playing the fish
best. Then release the tension until it is just pos-

sible to slip the clutch if the rod tip is raised higher, the equivalent of a downward pull by the fish.

If, as a fish is brought in for netting, too much line is retrieved so that the rod cannot be raised high enough for the fish to be slipped over the landing net then it will be necessary to release more line. If the fish is laying flat on the surface care must be taken as to how this extra line is given. In this case if the rod is pulled hard so that the clutch releases more line the energy required to start the clutch slipping may be enough to pull the hook from the mouth of the fish. It is safer to reverse the reel handle and allow more line out slowly and carefully.

When setting the tension of the clutch one should remember that it requires more effort to initially start the clutch slipping than to keep it slipping.

It is possible to play and net small fish successfully without any recourse to the slipping clutch. When bream fishing on occasions I have deliberately set the clutch tight and played the landed fish up to four pounds simply by using the action of the rod and the strength of line. However, this kind of fishing should be kept for experimenting.

When an angler is taking small fish of, say, up to two pounds, where he is able to reverse the reel handle and give off line if need be, he must decide for himself whether or not to use the clutch. To be perfectly safe, however, with any fish which can exert a pressure that approaches the danger tension for the line, the clutch should be used.

## PRACTICAL ILLUSTRATION

Let us imagine that we are bottom fishing for bream on a fairly wide river and intend to use a fixed-spool reel. To illustrate the points I have already made in this chapter let us try and visualise the scene as it may well happen.

The tackle includes a fourteen foot rod with stiffish action, a fixed-spool reel which has two spools, one containing $2\frac{1}{2}$ lb. line and the other containing 5 lb. line.

We tackle up as usual for light float leger fishing and try the lighter line first, tying to it a size 12 hook on 18 inch 4x bottom.

After tackling up but before casting out we fasten the hook to the rod rest which is firmly embedded in the bank and test the slipping clutch. With the rod at fifty degrees and the line taut we adjust the clutch so that a little extra pressure starts it slipping easily.

We bait up and cast out, mending line immediately because the slight side wind has taken out downstream a billow of line which will make striking difficult and tend to pull the float about with the run of water.

Soon the bream begin to feed and we strike at a good bite. At the strike the slipping clutch screeches because we have forgotten to place the right forefinger on the rim of the reel to prevent it slipping at the strike. It does not matter this time for the hook is home but had the fish been particularly large it might have run unbraked for a second or so before that important forefinger was placed on the reel spool.

The fish is cruising up and down in the swim neither taking nor giving line and if we wind the reel handle holding the rod in the same position the clutch simply slips and no gain of line is made. So the reel handle is wound only as the rod tip is slightly lowered and immediately a gain of line is made.

The fish pulls with a sudden renewal of effort and the clutch screeches into action again and once more the finger brakes. The pumping action is repeated as the rod tip is gently lowered and then raised again bringing the fish in closer. Soon he turns on his side and is slid into the net.

The next strike is made with the finger braking the reel spool so that the clutch will not give until the fish rushes off. This time the fish goes like a train straight up the river. We cannot feel his head shaking through the line and rightly assume that he is foulhooked as often happens in a crowded bream swim. The fish is hooked in the dorsal fin and as he has almost complete freedom he fights well. He rushes towards a weed patch to the right and, braking with the finger, we give side pressure to try and turn him. The fish is virtually lifted to the top of the water but when he wags his tail and goes down he turns round in the right direction.

This fish fights right up to the net and when he sees it he makes another bid for freedom. This time the clutch lets him go so that we can recoup a little and position the rod better for the netting. This time the rod butt is put down in front of the basket so that nothing will impede it if the rod must be moved again.

The fish is netted and safe, thanks to the efficiency of the clutch without which a break in line would have occurred as the fish broke away from the landing net on the first occasion. Then, the left hand was holding the net so that any line to be given had to go through the slipping clutch. Once again it prevented the loss of a good fish.

One or two bream escape later when they dive for the weeds near the opposite bank and it is virtually impossible to stop them. The clutch does not allow line breakage but the lightness of line does not let us turn the fish in time so we change to the other spool which contains five pound line.

This fresh tackle takes but a few moments to fit up but this time we have to increase the clutch tension slightly because of the increased line strength when we give it our test.

This heavier tackle allows us to manhandle the fish more but as the hook length is not so strong as the line we must still be careful.

Playing the fish on this line is sporting but not so risky as on lighter line and therefore not so exciting. The clutch does not need to slip so often and the rod handles the fish well.

There are two points of view, of course, concerning the weight of lines for this type of fishing. It may be considered necessary to use heavy lines to eliminate by sheer strength of tackle the possibility of lost fish. On the other hand there are those who would prefer using the lightest possible line and then, backed by the slipping clutch of the fixed-spool reel, use all their skill to net the fish. There is far more satisfaction to be gained in the latter school.

The slipping clutch assists the angler to use light lines which provide many more thrills in

angling than over-heavy lines. The clutch does
not prevent large fish from breaking absurdly
light tackle but then the bottom fisher who knows
his reel is sensible enough not to press his luck
too far.

# CHAPTER IV

## HEAVY TACKLE CASTING

OF all the forms of angling which the fixed-spool reel has encouraged match fishing and spinning must take pride of place. It would be fair to say that the reel has revolutionised both of these forms of fishing. I have already dealt with the practice of light tackle casting and fishing with the reel, as it applies to bottom fishing and match fishing. This chapter will deal with heavier fishing.

There are two main types of rod used for presenting a lure over a long distance, the two-handed long rod, similar in length to the bottom rod but not in action, and the short, light rod.

## DOUBLE-HANDED RODS

The first type of rod, the double-handed long rod is used for a variety of purposes in conjunction with the reel. It may be for salmon spinning, pike spinning, sea fishing and sea spinning. Whatever the requirement the action is only slightly modified each time and the cast with the reel is the manoeuvre with which we are concerned. In salmon spinning the lure may be a small spinner or devon minnow or a plug; in pike fishing the lure may be a large spinner, small spinner, dead bait or live-bait; in sea fishing the terminal tackle may hold a lure, heavy sea leads or float tackle.

64

The reel will work effectively in any of these combinations provided that the rod is suited to the weight of the lure and that the reel is correctly backed with line—always assuming that the correct cast is made.

The cast with the long rod using a fairly heavy bait, such as a dead bait, large spinner or live-bait is a slow, deliberate action which must be undertaken carefully because of the weight of tackle concerned.

It is obvious that a long rod with slight dimensions cannot satisfactorily perform this duty because it will give considerably and may even break in the action of casting. The type of rod designed for this work is generally made of built-cane, steel or glass.

Heavier tackle calls for heavier lines which in turn demand more space on the reel spool. Most fixed-spool reels of quality are sold with two spools, one for light lines and the other for heavier lines. There are, of course, the larger reels for sea fishing which are capable of holding lines up to thirty pounds breaking strain.

## CASTING

The cast with heavier tackle is very similar to the two-handed cast with light tackle, except that it must be more deliberate with good follow-through action.

The line is adjusted so that the bait hangs down about one third of the distance from the rod tip. The right hand holds the rod just above where the reel is seated and the left hand holds the rod lower down on the butt. As in the other casts the right forefinger retains the line when the pick-up arm is opened out in the extended position. In light tackle casting it may be only necessary to press the line against the rim of the spool but with heavier tackle there is always the danger of the tackle weight pulling the line away from the finger so it is best to totally encompass the line with the finger.

The position of the feet in this cast depend on whether the angler casts overhead or sideways. For the overhead cast the feet should oe set apart facing forwards and the top of the body swung as the rod is taken back over the shoulder.

As the rod is brought round over the shoulder the bait swings round behind the angler and as the rod is lowered or extended behind the angler so does the tackle extend further behind. The distance the angler droops his rod over his shoulder determines to some extent the distance to be achieved by the cast. The angler then slightly raises both hands to face level and with a steady throw ejects the bait over his head, as in Fig. 16.

The overhead cast is not the best cast for various reasons when using heavy items of tackle, items much heavier than a large spinner. It is useful then where obstacles may make a sideways cast impossible but the side cast, either right or left hand is the most accurate and easier of the two casts.

For the side cast the right foot is placed forward of the left foot if the cast is to be from the left side so that the angler is half facing his left. The swing back with the tackle as in the overhead cast is made but the angler can watch the action of his lure all the time, and can swing the bait up away from him to help the cast which

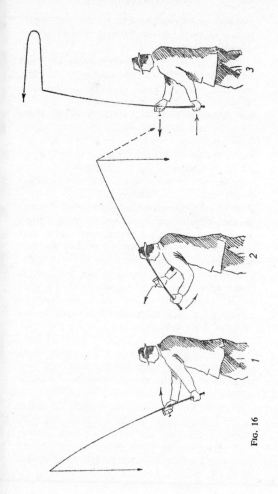

FIG. 16

follows. The follow-through as the rod comes round to the front of the body should be deliberate.

The same cast can be done from the right hand side but this time the position of the feet will be changed around. Accuracy in these casts is important and while many anglers find that the carefully performed sideways cast, often with the body completely sideways to the water, gives excellent accuracy, others find accuracy only when they cast from behind or at an angle of 45 degrees to the front of the body. They can thus face the front but modify the overhead two-handed cast to suit themselves.

With a double-handed rod a great deal depends on the individual preference and although anglers are inclined to follow a casting tutor rigidly it is well worthwhile to experiment to find the cast which suits the angler best.

The release of the line from the forefinger is often tricky for beginners who either release too late or too soon so that the tackle drops to the floor before it can be moved through the air or jerks around behind them or into the water at their feet.

The exact point of release is something which must be judged first and then becomes instinctive as different casts are tried and different directions sought.

Occasionally trouble arises because the tackle is not suitably matched and the angler may be trying to cast too light a lure with too large a rod. This calls for either an increase in the size and weight of the lure or an addition of weight on to the trace.

In any case it is of the utmost importance for the angler to have a reel spool correctly filled so that the line will flow out easily on casting.

## SHORT RODS

The cast using a short, whippy rod designed to cast very light lures is a one-handed cast. Most of the rods designed for this type of work are between five to nine feet in length and are made from quality built-cane, steel or glass. They are instruments of great precision when used correctly with the fixed-spool reel.

Great accuracy can, of course, be obtained with light bottom tackle and a fairly good tip action but in the short bait casting rod the angler is closer to this tackle and he can concentrate on accuracy all the time without having to bother about position of hands or feet.

More than ever when using this type of rod a correctly loaded reel becomes of paramount importance and it is because reels are not always kept up to top capacity that accuracy can drop off during a season.

The cast with the fixed-spool reel and the short rod brings into action the strongest arm of the angler, depending on whether he is right or left handed. The right handed angler can cast from his right as he would with the longer heavier rod or he can cast overhead or across his body and use only one hand if he wishes.

The cast action is virtually the same as described in chapter two if both hands are used and the rod swung sideways but there is no need for the deliberation required as in the cast with heavier tackle. The light lure should be virtually flicked out. If the cast is single-handed and overhead the rod is simply tipped back over the shoulder and a forward flick made in the required direction. The angler, once the cast is mastered, can fix his eyes rigidly on his aiming spot and when the lure shoots into his line of vision he can check the distance by the usual method of applying forefinger to reel drum, following this with closing down the pick-up arm into the action position.

Rods and reels which are properly matched will give long distance, accurate casing but occasionally a little more effort from the rod may help achieve distance. When this is so the light rod can be helped considerably by the left hand which takes up a position below the reel as in the long rod cast.

Having learned how to cast with the reel for spinning we must consider the use of the reel for this type of fishing.

## STRIKING

To be effective this reel must be adjusted so that when a strike is made the hooks drive home and yet it must still allow a fish to take line without breaking.

The adjustment for spinning should be similar in bottom fishing so that the fish can be played by finger pressure on the reel but where pike are concerned it may be necessary to strike a second time to drive home the hooks.

This is best illustrated when light tackle spinning for pike. A sudden impact on the lure shows that a pike has taken. If the fish closes its mouth on the lure and then moves off the hooks may not penetrate at all unless the angler gives a definite strike in the opposite direction. If he does not, then the fish may well open its mouth, shake its head and spill out the lure which was only lightly held in the mouth by the closing of the jaws.

Once the fish is firmly hooked it can be played safely on the reel with the clutch allowing line to be taken and the finger braking on the drum as in light tackle fishing. The pumping action with the lowering of the rod to gain line must be made.

## PLAYING

Much has been written about playing large fish on fixed-spool reels, often by persons who have had little experience. The trend appears to be to suggest that it is a difficult and alarming experience; nothing could be further from the truth.

A large fish played on a centre-pin reel can, on occasion, run so hard that he causes over-run on the reel. This cannot happen with a fixed-spool reel. If the fish is hooked and he runs immediately he will not break the tackle if the clutch is set so as to allow him to take line, even though the angler may still, inadvertently, be winding in with the reel handle. Naturally, as soon as the fish runs like this the forefinger must come into play on to the reel spool to apply the braking pressure.

Now it has been said that if one exerts pressure on a fish that is taking line this will induce him to take more line and induce him to run further. In my experience this is not so. Any reasonably competent angler can handle fish on a fixed-spool reel and will be more likely to be successful with it if he has some centre-pin reel fishing experience.

It is, indeed, difficult to play a fish and land it without exerting pressure at the earliest possible moment and, although the slipping clutch will let off line under little pressure the tension of the line through the action of the rod must exert upward pressure on to the fish, so that it is difficult to see how one can remove all pressure on a fish after striking unless one points the rod directly at the fish and takes the pick-up arm off so that the line runs freely without impediment.

One of the crucial points in the playing of a fish taken on a spinner is the time immediately following the strike and the hooking of the fish. That is when the fish makes its first decided run and that is the moment when the angler's hands are still in the position of retrieving line.

The next movement, the braking of the reel spool, can be achieved by simply pushing the forefinger of the hand holding the rod forward on to the spool. The braking effect of the finger prevents line from being taken too rapidly, additional pressure either sideways or upwards should be brought to bear on the fish by using the rod. When boat fishing for pike a hooked fish will often run under the boat and the only rod pressure that can effectively be exerted is from above. Finger pressure on a reel spool at such times is often difficult to maintain for a number of reasons. At such moments when it is imperative for the fish to be stopped and it seems impossible to do this without breaking the line or snapping the rod the angler often feels the urge to grip the handle of the reel and wind in furiously. This, of course, is no help with a loosely set slipping clutch. The only effective means of braking on the fish is by a combination rod pressure and drum pressure.

# CHAPTER V

## HINTS ON GENERAL HANDLING

THIS chapter is quite short but is intended to be to the point on one or two matters relating to the use of the fixed-spool reel. As I have hinted in the Foreword the reel is still an object of suspicion to many anglers, notably those of the old school so carefully reared on the centre-pin reel.

In itself this does not really matter but it is important that young anglers who are learning to cast should not be warned off the fixed-spool reel simply because of prejudice on the part of their elders.

I believe every young angler, especially those keen to learn bottom fishing, should possess a fixed-spool reel but they should not rely entirely upon it. It is a reel designed for a specific purpose; to enable light tackle to be cast long distances accurately, the words "light" and "long" being, of course, relative to the fishing in question.

Every young angler should consider two reels, the fixed-spool and the centre-pin, as essential parts of his equipment. He should fish with both, giving way to the centre-pin on narrow waters where long trotting is required or on any waters where, in fact, he need not cast further than he can manage with his centre-pin reel. This is the original reel of the bottom fisherman and is the best tool for this job.

So far as the fixed-spool reel is concerned the young angler should choose his reel carefully, not only for line capacity, sturdiness and general engineering efficiency but for grace of design and simple, practical points such as whether or not the reel is too small for anything more than child's play. Unfortunately, some cheap reels are far too small even for youngsters still at school. These reels depend on the collision between the bale-arm and part of the reel seating to complete the pick-up action and bring the bale-arm into play. This often means that the space between the bale-arm and the reel seating is small— enough, perhaps, for a very small set of fingers but far too small for an average-sized hand.

I have seen men with outsize hands using these reels and when they have held the rod above the reel the latter has virtually disappeared, leaving no room at all for the reel to work correctly. Such reels are useful because they offer a type of fixed-spool reel at a cheap price but they should be considered merely as stepping stones between the angler and the better-priced, more efficient and larger reels.

## LINE LOADS

Some of these reels will only work correctly if their spools are loaded to the brim with the lightest of lines. After a line break and consequent loss of line resulting in the line dropping below the rim of the spool casting often becomes a torment and the young angler has to impart a great deal of energy to throwing the line off the spool so that it literally jumps over the rim.

This is mechanically bad practice but is common among young anglers. Additionally the very small reels are used for the double role of light tackle casting and pike fishing when they are loaded with heavyweight lines. This often results in unholy tangles and great strain on the working parts of the reel. Heavy pike |fishing should be reserved for reels built to cope with this.

All these difficulties tend to put the young angler off when it is possible to use carefully and successfully even the cheapest type of fixed-spool reel, provided that the spool is correctly loaded as earlier described and the angler does not expect too much from his reel.

## THE ROD FOR THE REEL

The rod should be suited to the reel as far as possible. Young anglers tend to use decrepit rods which are not suitable for any form of fishing except that where the line is tied direct to the rod tip.

The adult angler who is often called in to advise the youngster on his choice of rod and reel should carefully think of these points and strive to match the two items of tackle carefully, bearing in mind the type of water the boy will fish.

It is often claimed by young anglers that their fixed-spool reels will allow them to fish any method, even long trotting at the rod tip, so that a centre-pin reel is not needed. While this book is devoted to the use of the fixed-spool reel I would never suggest that there is any reel so eminently suited to long-trotting as the centre-pin reel. This is virtually the perfect instrument, simply a wheel which picks up line.

## LONG TROTTING

I remember watching Billy Lane, of Coventry, one of our most famous match anglers, fishing the first Hampshire Avon Championship. He was trotting a swim at his rod tip and using a centre-pin reel. Elsewhere other anglers were fishing similar swims with fixed-spool reels.

I commented on this and suggested that he found the flaw in the fixed-spool reel in such conditions was when he wished to retrieve. The tackle would peel line off the loaded spool well enough without any hindrance but when a strike was made and a fish hooked he had then to hold the line tight until the pick-up arm was brought over by winding the reel handle forward.

Billy agreed and said that at such distances a hooked fish would escape if the line was allowed to slacken for only a second. When using the centre-pin reel the angler merely stops the movement of reel drum with a finger and strikes at the same time. The retrieve follows without any further delaying movement or mechanical process either by winding in with the left hand or revolving the reel drum by hitting it with the palm of the hand.

The flip-over type of pick-up arm, now used in the Mitchell reel, helps to remove this fault when the strike has been made and the fish is to be reeled in. The bale-arm is flipped over easily by one finger, a quicker process than having to bring over the reel handle; nevertheless it still has to be performed and takes time.

It seems virtually impossible to strike after putting forward the bale-arm pick-up because this would mean that the handle of the reel would have to be brought forward as the float indicates a bite before the strike was made. By this method fish would seldom be hooked. The action must always be that the finger holds the line either against the spool or against the rod as the strike is made. This grip must not be slackened before the fish is reeled in because any slackening will enable the fish to throw the hook, especially in fast water when the fish is hooked at some distance from the angler.

Any young angler who requires first-hand experience of the difficulty I have outlined should practice long-trotting with both reels.

## SEA CASTING

In earlier chapters I have made little reference to sea fishing with the reel because the casts dealt with in the chapter on heavy tackle casting apply to sea fishing. The principle of casting is the same, only the tackle changes. However, there are occasions when sea fishing, such as in a boat, when it may be difficult to use a fixed-spool reel.

I have seen the reel used in a crowded boat by anglers fishing for tope and although I would not advocate the reel for this type of fishing it can be used. In cramped conditions a short rod is ideal because it will allow a strong cast to be made, putting the tackle some distance away from the boat. This cast may have to be made from a sitting, standing or kneeling position.

The angler should very carefully observe the amount of space there is behind him so that his backswing will not hit anyone. If possible the swing should be achieved with the rod held out over the boat so that the cast becomes practically a side cast. If the rod is whippy the backswing can be short but invariably the terminal tackle will climb high on release and aiming may be rather difficult.

From a beach, casting is much easier, as it is from a pier, because a long rod can be used and the two-handed cast utilised. I have seen the cast made by a sea angler with the terminal tackle actually resting on the shore, but the best casts, from a distance point of view, are made when the terminal tackle is swung out and hanging from the rod end. After the cast the rod is either held or placed in a rest. The angler using a centre-pin reel for beach fishing usually loops the line over the reel handle to hold it tight against the sea movement because often the mere action of the check is not enough to prevent line from being taken away.

With a fixed-spool reel the check will usually prevent the line from pulling the reel spool round to release more line and for anything less than specimen fish it will not be necessary to have the slipping clutch tension very low.

Most beach-caught sea fish can be brought in steadily with a winding-in of the reel. Notable exceptions are tope, skate, and conger, but whatever the species, if there is the chance of a sudden tightening of the line and breakage of tackle, the slipping clutch should be eased off considerably. The retrieving procedure is the pumping action described in Chapter III.

On the subject of the fixed-spool reel as used by the sea angler I should add here that it is imperative when using the fixed-spool reel to know the mechanics of the particular reel you are using. If the reel is borrowed it should be correctly set before you take it over and checked to ensure that it works correctly.

Occasionally, a newcomer to the reel will carefully unwind the tension on the slipping clutch after casting only to find that he has loosened the spool assembly so that it comes to pieces in his hand. He should make certain first how to adjust the clutch and by how much for the line he is using.

## USING THE SLIPPING CLUTCH

The final part of this book should serve to emphasise to all users of the fixed-spool reel that the slipping clutch is well worth understanding and worth using.

It has been said that any fish can be caught on a fixed-spool reel on light lines if the clutch is used correctly. This is not true. Captain Terry Thomas, in his recent book *Casting*, rightly points out that this opinion does not take into account any obstacles in the swim.

The slipping clutch allows the angler to play the fish by giving the fish line without possibility of line breakage. All line given to a fish must be reclaimed before the fish can be netted, a point worth considering before and during fishing. No angler should give line unless he is forced to do so. Often a fish will make an initial run and take off a good deal of line. If the swim is clear of obstacles then the angler has a chance to retrieve his line but if there are obstacles in the swim he must exert pressure on the fish to keep him clear of them.

Any sensible fish knows the obstacles which will help him and fish such as chub and tench make for lily pads and tree roots in a twinkling when hooked. Sometimes a great deal of pressure on the fish will move it, more often than not the fish will sulk and move only after the pressure is removed entirely.

This is usually rod tip pressure and not pressure exerted by the angler through the reel when the fish is in free motion and swimming hard. It is, of course, better to have the clutch completely eased off than merely slightly eased because there are chances of line breaks if the fish runs and the clutch is tighter than it should be. The finger on the reel spool controls the release of line to the fish and applies the tension to slow him down.

The angler unversed in the use of the reel will often merely hold the reel handle as the clutch screams out, and very often he will wind against the run of the fish so that he is needlessly winding and the fish is still taking line out quite easily because of the clutch's low tension.

A further word about very light line fishing. It is now a regular practice on some rivers to fish at long distances, using a fixed-spool reel and three or four pound line. This means that the strike into the fish is made at a long distance.

The breaking strain of the line is diminished in water and if it is very light a strong strike may result in a break just above the float where the line is soaked below and dry above. Many anglers prefer to fish with the tension of the clutch set very low so that when a strike is made some of the energy is absorbed by the clutch.

This reduces the chances of the line breaking when a reasonable fish is hooked, although it may well be argued that it reduces to a certain degree the penetrating power of the hook. This is bound to be so, however, when such light lines are used.

## THE ENCLOSED SPOOL REEL

This book would not be complete (writes the author) without some reference to the enclosed spool or closed-face reel, of which there are now a number appearing on the British market. The reel is considered by many to be the fixed-spool reel of the future and, despite some advantages, it is certain to become popular over here.

The reel, already popular in the United States and on the Continent, has the line spool fully enclosed, the line leaving the reel through a small hole in the casing. The immediate advantage of this is that once the line is on the spool and threaded through its escape hole it need not be handled by the angler when casting.

Inside the enclosure the line is wound round a spool similar to the normal open spool on the fixed-spool reel, the pick-up arm being a small upright piece of metal attached to the moveable spool front. This front portion of the spool revolves when the handle is moved and takes round the pick-up which winds the line onto the spool. The whole of this is enclosed by the metal sheath which streamlines the reel.

The pick-up is operated in various ways. On some reels it is put down (so that the line is able to leave the spool during a cast) by the reel handle being jerked back against its normal winding direction. On other reels a trigger operated by the forefinger is used which must be depressed at the correct moment during the cast.

These reels are obviously very useful for the handling of fine lines and are so set that the smallest motion pulls line off the line spool. With thicker lines there are certain problems, not the least of which is a limit in the amount of line the spool will hold.

From a mechanical point of view this reel does not conform with the specifications I gave for the perfect fixed-spool reel in an earlier chapter. Theoretically the perfect reel should function in casting and yet the amount of resistance met by the line when under pressure should be at a minimum. Hence my suggestion for the metal in the arm-crook of the normal fixed-spool bale-arm to be moveable as the line passes over it under pressure. On the enclosed fixed-spool reel the line is drawn from immediately beneath the pick-up arm and is set at right angles to its spool position within a short distance. The pick-up also exercises great pressure directly on the line with no modification of the angle between the line on the spool and the line leaving the reel. This is unavoidable because whatever other principles the reel uses it must use acute angles for line handling in order to contain this mechanism inside the limits of the spool enclosure.

Nevertheless there will be many anglers who prefer a smooth looking reel with no excresances such as bale-arm pick-ups. They will also appreciate not having to touch the line once it is within the reel where it is adequately protected from the weather. Trotting the stream, using such a reel is made extremely easy, provided that fine lines are used. Casting with fine lines is also very comfortable and great accuracy can be attained.

# CHAPTER VI

By Barrie Welham, *International Casting Champion and Record Holder. Mr. Welham holds the European record with fixed-spool reel, single-handed rod and ⅜ oz. bait with a cast of 90 yards and 6 ins. Scarborough, 1956. This tackle is, of course, very similar to that used by the average coarse fisherman so that he is particularly qualified to comment on this type of casting.*

To come in at the end of a book which has already comprehensively dealt with such a specialised subject as the fixed spool reel is not an easy task.

The only opportunity which is clearly open to me, is to touch briefly on some of the techniques which are used by competitive casters and which, as they became second nature to me, proved to be useful in my actual fishing.

I think the most important thing that tournament casting taught me, is the importance of familiarity with one's equipment. This is true with every type of tackle outfit but especially so with the fixed spool reel. To cast with a stationary drum reel must be one of the most easily mastered of all casting techniques, but the number of physical movements prior to the actual line release is more than with any other fishing reel. To acquire the dexterity needed for quick, smooth and certain manipulation of the reel is a thing which only absolute familiarity with your tackle will give.

The way in which the index finger picks up the line and the bale arm is opened and later, how the index finger reaches out and gently feels for the lip of the drum restricting the flow of line so that bait and float enter the water completely under control. This manipulative dexterity in the use of the reel comes from practice due to familiarity but good casting is a little more than just that.

Before going on to the cast itself, let us just touch on one part of the tackle which has a great influence on the result. Due to the very principle by which the fixed spool operates, the rings have a much greater influence on this reel than on any other. The way in which the line spirals from the spool makes the use of a large diameter butt ring very desirable. For use with a reel of freshwater dimensions this ring, which will begin the task of breaking down the coil of line, should have an internal diameter of at least $\frac{3}{4}''$ and better still an 1". It should not be too close to the reel or the line will bunch up before it gets through. Conversely, if the ring is too far up the rod it will not control the flapping action along the rod which arises from the momentum of the line spiralling over the lip of the spool. Experiments and high speed photography have shown that the best position for a ring of 1" diameter standing $\frac{1}{2}''$ off to the bottom edge is between 18"—24" from the face of the spool. The number of other rings on a rod is also of considerable importance because the line is still whirling for some distance up the rod and insufficient rings allows this to continue up to and even through the tip-top. So although the use of sufficient rings is really necessitated by the demand to distribute the load throughout the rod when under stress, they are also needed for line control. A standard 7 ft. spinning rod to be really adequately ringed needs as many as six intermediate and a tip-top making seven in all. While on the subject of light casting spinning rods it is worthwhile remembering that the rings should also be light. There is little if any strain on them; they should be of adequate diameter made of light fine wire neatly brazed into a light wire bridge. The rings when mounted should be positioned to lie one inside the other right through from butt to tip when viewed from a position just above the butt.

When it comes to the cast itself, the only thing I can add to that already written, is about the picking up of the line from the corner of the bale arm when this is in the uppermost position. When the index finger reaches down it should take the line across the centre of the ball and I then prefer to take it right up and into the corner formed by the rod mounting and the reel stem. If you prefer two fingers on either side of the reel the line will go into the corner at the side of the middle finger. But in either place, the line is very firmly and positively trapped even if the finger is so wet and cold as to be numb, or if stiffened by advancing years. The more usual way in which the line lies across the partially extended forefinger can allow it to be released prematurely. The method of trapping the line at the lip of the spool is very sensitive and releases very cleanly, but in cold weather or if casting rather heavy floats with some vigour, the other way seems more positive. You will notice that earlier it was said that the line should be across the ball of the finger.

Often the line is taken across the first joint but this can never be released so smoothly and in consequence the accuracy of the casting is jeopardised.

## LONG CASTING

If at some time you are in the rare position where you consider long casting is necessary these few final thoughts may help. Make sure that you have your spools filled correctly and use the finest line commensurate with the weight being used and the power of your rod. Choose the line carefully, some makes are much thinner for equal breaking strain than others. Prior to making a really long cast it will help if you wind the reel so that the spool is fully forward and clear of the revolving flyer as the line does tend to flap a little if the spool is deep inside. This applies more to some reels than to others. The last point is that with a light bait some advantage is gained by having a long over-hang. This increases the casting arch which in turn increases momentum.

I should like to end with a personal word to all users or prospective users of the fixed spool reel. Used properly they are a sheer delight to fish with and over the years the automatic action which makes for this delight will certainly come to you; but these reels are designed as much for the novice as the expert and there is a considerable margin for initial error. By attention to detail you can increase your angling pleasure but even without that care the bait will still get there effortlessly—somehow!

# APPENDIX

## DIAMETER AND BREAKING STRAIN OF NYLON

Various makes of nylon differ a little in the relationship of diameter to breaking strain, but the following is a fair guide.

| Diameter | Breaking Strain | Equivalent in x gut sizes |
|---|---|---|
| 0.004″ | 3 lb. | — |
| 0.005″ | 1½ lb. | 8x |
| 0.006″ | 2¼ lb. | 6x |
| 0.007″ | 3 lb. | 4x |
| 0.008″ | 4 lb. | 3x |
| 0.009″ | 5 lb. | 2x |
| 0.010″ | 6 lb. | 1x |
| 0.011″ | 7 lb. | 0x |
| 0.012″ | 9 lb. | 9/5 |
| 0.013″ | 10 lb. | 8/5 |
| 0.014″ | 12 lb. | 7/5 |
| 0.016″ | 15½ lb. | 5/5 |
| 0.018″ | 19 lb. | 3/5 |
| 0.020″ | 23 lb. | 1/5 |
| 0.022″ | 28 lb. | — |

# INDEX